Joanne

Happy Birthday
and luck, health
and happiness
for every day of the
coming years.
Love,
Lillian
11/13/95

CATS

A
BOOK OF
DAYS

Playing with His Favorite Pet

CATS

A
BOOK OF
DAYS

Great Pond Publishing

Cats: A Book of Days
Copyright © 1992 Bluewood Books

This edition published in 1992 by NDM Publications, Inc.
Great Pond Publishing is an imprint of:
NDM Publications, Inc.
30 Inwood Road
Rocky Hill, CT 06067

Produced by
Bluewood Books
A Division of The Siyeh Group, Inc.,
P.O. Box 460313
San Francisco, CA 94146
ISBN 1-56657-024-7

Printed in Hong Kong

My Cat and I

With Persian cat beside my cheek,
Our mirrored counterpart we seek.
In servile glass we view a pair
With shining mass of amber hair,
White avid nails, and cruel grace
Of snuggling curves, and piquant face,
And topaz eyes that cannot cry;
Demure and sleek, my cat and I.

Not love nor work, our purring dream,
But cushioned warmth and clotted cream.
In stealthy games, not played by rules,
We dally with bewildered fools,
Amused to see them squirm and die; . . .
Caressed and fed, my cat and I.

—Edna Gearhart

My Kitty © Bluewood Archives

January

25

26

27

28

29

30

31

On a Night of Snow

Cat, if you go outdoors you must walk in the snow.
You will come back with little white shoes on your feet,
Little white slippers of snow that have heels of sleet.
Stay by the fire, my Cat. Lie still, do not go.
See how the flames are leaping and hissing low,
I will bring you a saucer of milk like a marguerite,
So white and so smooth, so spherical and so sweet—
Stay with me, Cat. Outdoors the wild winds blow.

Outdoors the wild, winds blow, Mistress, and dark is the night.
Strange voices cry in the trees, intoning strange lore,
And more than cats move, lit by our eyes' green light,
On silent feet where the meadow grasses hang hoar—
Mistress, there are portents abroad of magic and might,
And things that are yet to be done. Open the door!

—Elizabeth Coatsworth

February

1

2

3

4

5

kot europejski

Polska

1.55 ZŁ

J. GRABIANSKI

PWPW

Kot Europejski

J. Grabianski

February

6

7

8

9

10

February

11

12

13

14

15

16

17

Sin Shu

February

18

19

20

21

22

23

24

February

25

26

27

28

29

Musing, I sit on my cushioned settle,
    Facing the firelight's fitful shine;
Sings on the hob the simmering kettle,
    Songs that seem echoes of "auld lang syne."

And close beside me the cat sits purring,
    Warming her paws at the cheery gleam;
The flames keep flitting and flicking and whirring,
    My mind is lapped in a realm of dream.

—Heinrich Heine

A Mother and Her Kitten

March

1

2

3

4

5

March

6

7

8

9

10

March

11

12

13

14

15

16

17

The Owl and the Pussycat

18
....

19
....

20

From

The Owl and the Pussy Cat

The Owl and the Pussy Cat went to sea
    In a beautiful pea green boat;
They took some honey and plenty of money
    Wrapped up in a five pound note.
The Owl looked up to the stars above,
    And sang to a small guitar,
"O lovely Pussy, O Pussy, my love,
    What a beautiful Pussy you are,
        You are,
        You are!
    What a beautiful Pussy you are!"

Pussy said to the Owl, "You elegant fowl,
    How charmingly sweet you sing!
Oh! let us be married; too long we have tarried:
    But what shall we do for a ring?"
They sailed away, for a year and a day,
    To the land where the bong tree grows;
And there in a wood, a Piggy-wig stood,
    With a ring at the end of his nose,
        His nose,
        His nose,
    With a ring at the end of his nose.

"Dear Pig, are you willing to sell for one shilling
    Your ring?" Said the Piggy, "I will."
So they took it away, and were married next day
    By the Turkey who lives on the hill.
They dined on mince, and slices of quince,
    Which they ate with a runcible spoon,
And hand in hand, on the edge of the sand,
    They danced by the light of the moon,
        The moon,
        The moon,
    They danced by the light of the moon.

                    —Edward Lear

March

21

22

23

24

March

25

26

27

28

29

30

31

Hercules ©Lynn Van Couvering Uribe

April

1

2

3

4

5

April

6

7

8

9

10

April

11

12

13

14

15

16

17

April

18

19

20

21

22

23

24

April

25

26

27

28

29

30

I have a little pussy,
    And her coat is silvery gray;
She lives in a great wide meadow,
    And she never runs away.
She always is a pussy;
    She'll never be a cat,
Because—she's a pussy willow!
    Now what do you think of that?

—*Traditional*

A Lady and Her Cat

May

. . . .

1
. . . .

2
. . . .

3
. . . .

4
. . . .

5

May

6

7

8

9

10

May
. . . .

11
. . . .

12
. . . .

13
. . . .

14
. . . .

15
. . . .

16
. . . .

17

May

. . . .

18

. . . .

19

. . . .

20

. . . .

21

. . . .

22

. . . .

23

. . . .

24

May

....

25
....

26
....

27
....

28
....

29
....

30
....

31

To an Enchantress

Little gray wonder, in pride of fur,
Start up your wheel, with its pebbly whirr,
And spin me a twilight's length of purr.

Oh, the many I've courted of variant hue,
Tigers and blacks and a Malta blue!
But never, oh, never! a one like you.

Swish me that tail and its madding curl
Of the quivering tip, with a gamesome twirl:
For the sleet's abroad and the leaves a-whirl.

Then, when the rumple-some wind flies higher,
Scud, ere your pinky pads can tire,
To cushioned ease by the leaping fire.

Close up your topaz eyes and dream,
Paw over nose, of a witch-fire's gleam,
Of Pharaohs mummied and morning cream, —

Of the long, long road you have traveled down
From the sunrise Sphinx and the crumbled throne
To a hearthside realm that is all your own.

—Alice Brown

June

1

2

3

4

5

Kot Perski   J. Grabiański

June

6

7

8

9

10

June

11

12

13

14

15

16

17

June

18

19

20

21

22

23

24

Breaking the News

June

25

26

27

28

29

30

Careful observers may foretell the hour
(By sure prognostics) when to dread a shower;
While rain depends, the pensive cat gives o'er
Her frolics, and pursues her tail no more.

—Jonathan Swift

A Serious Question

A kitten went a-walking
One morning in July
And idly fell a-talking
With a great big butterfly.

The kitten's tone was airy,
The butterfly would scoff;
When there came along a fairy
Who whisked his wings right off.

And then—for it is written
Fairies can do such things—
Upon the startled kitten
She stuck the yellow wings.

The kitten felt a quiver,
She rose into the air,
Then flew down to the river
To view her image there.

With fear her heart was smitten,
And she began to cry:
"Am I a butter-kitten?
Or just a kitten-fly?"

—Carolyn Wells

July

....

1
....

2
....

3
....

4
....

5

July

6

7

8

9

10

July

....

11

....

12

....

13

....

14

....

15

....

16

....

17

Ditto with Bougainvillea

July

18

19

20

21

22

23

24

July

25

26

27

28

29

30

31

Verses on a Cat

A cat in distress,
Nothing more, nothing less;
Good folks, I must faithfully tell ye,
As I am a sinner,
It wants for some dinner
To stuff out its own little belly.

You would not easily guess
All the modes of distress
Which torture the tenants of earth;
And the various evils
Which like so many devils,
Attend the poor souls from their birth.

Some a living require,
And others desire
An old fellow out of the way;
And which is the best
I leave to be guessed,
For I cannot pretend to say.

One wants society,
Another variety,
Others a tranquil life;
Some want food,
Others as good,
Only want a wife.

But this poor little cat
Only wanted a rat.
To stuff out its own little maw;
And it were as good
Some people had such food,
To make them *hold their jaw!*

—Percy Bysshe Shelley

Persian

August

1

2

3

4

5

August

. . . .

6

. . . .

7

. . . .

8

. . . .

9

. . . .

10

August

....

11

....

12

....

13

....

14

....

15

....

16

....

17

August

18

19

20

21

22

23

24

August

....

25

....

26

....

27

....

28

....

29

....

30

....

31

Little Kitty

Once there was a little kitty,
    White as the snow;
In a barn she used to frolic,
    Long time ago.

In the barn a little mousie
    Ran to and fro,
For she heard the little kitty,
    Long time ago.

Two black eyes had little kitty,
    Black as a sloe,
And they spied the little mousie,
    Long time ago.

Four soft paws had little kitty,
    Paws soft as snow,
And they caught the little mousie,
    Long time ago.

Nine pearl teeth had little kitty,
    All in a row,
And they bit the little mousie,
    Long time ago.

When the teeth bit little mousie,
    Mousie cried out, "Oh!"
But she slipped away from kitty,
    Long time ago.

—Elizabeth Prentiss

September

1

2

3

4

5

September

6

7

8

9

10

September

11

12

13

14

15

16

17

kot europejski

30 GR

Polska

Kot Europejski

J. Grabiański

September

. . . .

18

. . . .

19

. . . .

20

. . . .

21

. . . .

22

. . . .

23

. . . .

24

September

25

26

27

28

29

30

She moved through the garden in glory because
She had very long claws at the end of her paws.
Her back was arched, her tail was high,
A green fire glared in her vivid eye;
And all the Toms, though never so bold,
Quailed at the martial Marigold.

—Richard Garnett

My Cat

Deep in my brain walks to and fro,
As well as in his own domain,
A handsome cat of gentle strain,—
Scarce can I hear his mew so low.

His tender call wakes not alarm,
But though he growl or softly sound,
Still is his voice rich and profound,—
There lies his secret and his charm.

No other bow can ever bring
From my heart's perfect instrument
Such royal notes of deep content
Or waken its most vibrant string.

Than can thy voice, mysterious Puss,
Seraphic cat, and cat most strange,
As a celestial, scorning change,
As subtle as harmonious.

With growing wonderment I see
The fire in thy pale pupils glow
Like watch lights when the sun is low,
Thy living opals gaze at me.

—Pierre Charles Baudelaire

Me-ow Song

October

1

2

3

4

5

October

6

7

8

9

10

October

11

12

13

14

15

16

17

Floyd ©Lynn Van Couvering Uribe

October

18
. . . .

19
. . . .

20
. . . .

21
. . . .

22
. . . .

23
. . . .

24

October

25

26

27

28

29

30

31

The Tom Cat

At midnight in the alley
     A Tom cat comes to wail,
And he chants the hate of a million years
     As he swings his snaky tail.

Malevolent, bony, brindled,
     Tiger and devil and bard,
His eyes are coals from the middle of Hell
     And his heart is black and hard.

He twists and crouches and capers
     And bares his curved sharp claws,
And he sings to the stars of the jungle nights
     Ere cities were, or laws.

Beast from a world primeval,
     He and his leaping clan,
When the blotched red moon leers over the roofs,
     Give voice to their scorn of man.

He will lie on a rug tomorrow
     And lick his silky fur,
And veil the brute in his yellow eyes
     And play he's tame, and purr.

But midnight in the alley
     He will crouch again and wail,
And beat the time for his demon's song
     With the swing of his demon's tail.

—Don Marquis

Kitten with a Fan   © Sheila Fairchild

November

....

1
....

2
....

3
....

4
....

5

November

6

7

8

9

10

The Cat that Walked by Himself   Rudyard Kipling

HOLDING HER DOLLY.

Holding Her Dolly

November

11

12

13

14

15

16

17

November

18

19

20

21

22

23

24

November

25

26

27

28

29

30

Pussy cat, pussy cat, where have you been?
I've been to London to look at the Queen.
Pussy cat, pussy cat, what did you do there?
I frightened a little mouse under the chair.

—*English rhyme*

Tsuki   © Carol Rankin Takaki

December

1

2

3

4

5

December

6

7

8

9

10

Wish Birds Couldn't Fly

Stone Soup

December

11

12

13

14

15

16

17

December

18

19

20

21

22

23

24

To a Kitten

Did a fairy's fancy spin you,
　　Little cloud of silken fluff,
Or has fashions's whim decreed
　　An animated powder puff?

Cradled you are in my hand—
　　Pulsing flower of rumpled gloss—
Does a gauzy wisp of soul
　　Hide beneath such down and floss?

Ah! No blossom ever owned
　　Roguish stars for eyes; nor could
Cache such seedlet pearls within
　　A lined-with-pink snapdragon hood.

Ears like velvet shells that perk
　　Where forbidden tassels swing!
Toes like rosy berries where
　　Grow white thorns to snatch and cling!

Elfin whiskers which might be
　　The framework of a butterfly—
Are they strings on which the bow
　　Of contented purrs may ply?

Was your racing little heart,
　　Clothed in furred rotundity,
First conceived in jungle-gloom
　　And evolved—a gift for me?

　　　　　　　　　　—Rena M. Manning

Teddy

December

25

26

27

28

29

30

31

Victorian Cats